CITY OF HEY BABY

poems by

Patrice Melnick

Finishing Line Press
Georgetown, Kentucky

CITY OF HEY BABY

Copyright © 2020 by Patrice Melnick
ISBN 978-1-64662-336-5 First Edition
All rights reserved under International and Pan-American Copyright Conventions. No part of this book may be reproduced in any manner whatsoever without written permission from the publisher, except in the case of brief quotations embodied in critical articles and reviews.

ACKNOWLEDGMENTS

With gratitude to the publications in which these poems first appeared:

"Creole House" in *Drunken Boat*
"Dancing at Tipitina's After the Flood" in *Swamp Lily Review*
"Dancing at Tipitina's After the Flood," and "French Quarter Railings" in *Vision Verse*
"Tattoos and Birthmarks" in *Green Briar Review*
"Watermelon from the New Orleans Farmer's Market" in *Turning Up the Volume* (Xavier Review Press)

Publisher: Leah Huete de Maines
Editor: Christen Kincaid
Cover Art: Jerome Ford
Author Photo: Cheré Coen
Cover Design: Elizabeth Maines McCleavy

Order online: www.finishinglinepress.com
also available on amazon.com

Author inquiries and mail orders:
Finishing Line Press
P. O. Box 1626
Georgetown, Kentucky 40324
U. S. A.

Table of Contents

Dancing at Tipitina's After the Flood 1

French Quarter Railings, New Orleans 2

Dumaine St. 3

Fifty Days After Hurricane Katrina 4

Refrigerator Lesson 6

Rock n Bowl 7

How I Came to Understand Boudin 8

Magnifique 9

Ginger Blossoms 10

Creole House 12

Trash Day 13

Walking Through Palmetto Swamps 14

Comfort Post Katrina 15

Dead Woman Winter 16

Tattoos and Birthmarks 18

A Reporter Who Parties 19

Mathew 20

Lemon Sestina 22

Watermelon from the New Orleans Farmers Market 24

City of Hey Baby 26

*For Olan, forever a flame in my life.
Also, to the vibrant City of New Orleans;
her spirit lives in my soul.*

Dancing at Tipitina's after the Flood

My husband frowns because I don't stay home
anymore. Sunday afternoon, he is planting new
crepe myrtles, or painting over brown scum waterlines
that ring our house. I take off for Tip's to waltz in the arms
of "God knows who," Bernie says. "*Whom*," I correct
him. "You're wrong," he says, "it's who." Whatever.

Sundays at three, it's the Bruce Daigrepont band.
They've played every week since the children were really
children. April, 2006, Tip's reopens and I am there, like clockwork.
It's down the street past weary houses and yards of car corpses.
My best friend meets me there and we Cajun jitterbug with courteous
country boys and crazy, middle aged bachelors who ask
a different girl with every song. I spin 'til my vision tilts,
and I wear my fresh, post-Katrina now-I-can-dance skirt,
and my mind fogs over stale thoughts of bidding
building contractors and that dead end Road Home program.
Sunday, after three, no more putrid trash piles in the street and
no yellow barricade police ribbons around the suicide
house of the week.

I look over the rounded shoulder at my chin, and see a sea of used
up faces that just stare back. The dancers become a wave
of sweaty, mindless bodies that rock-sway, rock-sway into muddy
water. My nostrils fill with the scent of red beans and rice and stale
beer. Daigrepont's voice calls out; Gina Foresythe's fiddle cry cuts
back and forth above our heads and I sway in the blue
arms of "God knows whom."

French Quarter Railings

Finally Andrea hears your call, opens
the double doors onto her balcony.
She leans way over the wrought iron
railing, hand-rolled cigarette dangling
from her fingers and she tosses up a loud
Caribbean laugh that floats like a striped
beach ball at a Grateful Dead concert.

She drops the keys into your hands so
you can let yourself in through the street-level
door. Climb the stairs to enter this insomniac
apartment with the chartreuse-hued walls and
exhausted novels that lie scattered across the floor.
Andrea hands you a glass of red wine, blows smoke
into the air in this second floor flat of
chaos and freedom.

Dumaine Street

Across the street,
yo-yo guys
with pendulum attitudes
and money curled in pockets
like turning leaves.

Over there, whosh of midnight cars
watch your toes
close your doors
shut the shades
"Hello" means
too many things.

Fifty Days after Hurricane Katrina on Dumaine Street

1.
New Orleans is my old lover
from years ago whom I no longer care for
until I drive through the muddy city and
everyone waves to me, like folks do
in small towns and my eyes flood for
our years together.

2.
My house is a time capsule.
Unfolded laundry sleeps on the couch
one cast iron skillet grows green rings of mold.

In the tree-fallen yard, birds hush among
dead branches. The quiet I once wished for
feels forced and silence less peaceful
than I had imagined.

Ghosts of next door neighbors blast
Sunday gospel music.
In my memory, children squeal and pluck
sunflowers from strangers' gardens.
Before the storm, young men in thin white t-shirts
rocked on the corner and leaned into briefly parked cars.

3.
Squirrel whispers, sparrow chirps.
Do they live better without the revving
of car engines, without dumpster corn chips
and suspended trays of birdseed?

4.
I may lose my job
a change I'd considered for years.
Boxes lie partially packed.
When I unplug the stereo,
box up the Nevilles, Dr. John,
Johnny Adams, Irma Thomas
when I pack them, I will be finished here.

5.
Rotting animal carcass stenches the air and
grey ash coats trees and dry grass.
In the fork of a fallen pecan tree
one squirrel squat sits, frozen-eyed.
Was this the one that chased the others, fuss-barked
and stole bits from dog bowls? Squirrel fur trembles.
I step closer and it flees through brittle branches.
Before I leave the capsule, I pour left-over dog food
on the back porch.

6.
I used to walk down the street to buy a newspaper
then to La Boulangerie for a chocolate croissant
to carry home. *The Times-Picayune* spread across my Sunday table
sunlight spilled over the headlines. All morning I lingered
with croissant and tea with milk, sugar and an
African seed spice. Croissant, spiced tea,
the funnies.
I am visiting a place where I once lived.
I am visiting the person I used to be.

Refrigerator Lesson

After Hurricane Katrina, all
the refrigerators in town turned
sour, became petri dish canisters
cooking raw sides of meat
gently rotting fish, simmering tubs
of sour cream.

The only thing to do for
your internally blossoming
fridge was to duct tape it shut
like a rancid clam. You must
learn to roll it to the street
park it by the curb for pickup.

I still dream every night of mountains
of closed clams baking in the south
Louisiana sun. Think of ripening meats and
dented metal boxes
bursting with despair.

Rock n Bowl

Dear Rock n Bowl,
Your bowling lanes
are uneven and that Zydeco
music blasts like a throbbing
furnace while the 2nd floor
wooden planks give beneath
the synchronized pounding
heels of cowboy boots.

How can I thank you?

How I Came to Understand Boudin

At 7 a.m. on a chilly Mardi Gras trail
ride in Soileau, Louisiana I sit in the open hay
wagon with other horseless riders shivering
from the February cold, many of us wrapped
in blankets, wearing costumes of gold, purple and green.
Long line of horses and pickup trucks winds through
the frost-glazed countryside. As bitter breezes nip
my neck, a round faced, freckled woman pulls out
a paper bag of boudin and passes the stuff around
and I take a piece, hold the link between my fingers.
The ricey pork sausage warms my hand, is soft, fatty,
satisfying with each bite. Tiny cayenne kick,
texture on the tongue, warms lips and throat,
becomes a blanket on the inside. The line slows,
everyone jumps out and a trio plays La Chanson
de Mardi Gras. We zydeco dance and the morning swirls
with color, music and warm boudin that holds
winter reality at bay.

Magnifique

I saw you that day
at the last minute before
the Carrollton bus
took off, that bus
with waves of black stuff
exhausting out the back,
so magnifique,
like the plume
blowing out of your
lovely chapeau. I didn't
think you would catch
that bus.

I mean, how can anyone so
out of sorts, sorting through
your spare change, in those horse-clopping
shoes, hair over your eyes, how
could you catch anything
much less a rocking bus
side-to-side?

But to everyone's surprise,
you leapt to that bottom
step just before
the doors shut tight like
elevator doors, your last
high heel just landing
and you got all closed up
in that cool-conditioning
and I know you were the most
dismayed to be aboard
and I thought to myself,
what a move!

Ginger Blossoms
Ruth Mable Norwood Harris
December 20, 1904 – October 16, 1999

That morning we snipped blooming ginger stalks
        divided up the shell-white blossoms
        and placed fragrant shoots
        into water-filled vases.

No one spoke
        of how each cluster would scent the air
        as the crow of the iridescent-plumed rooster
        that you gathered in your arms for years.

No mention of how waves of fragrance would
        paint the rooms of our memories,
        how your spirit would echo your love
        of summer swelter
        echo love of digging hands into warm earth
        urging bright growth.

But we knew fingers of ginger flowers
        would thread the air
        like stitches through a sister's hem
        like stitches through young son's sleeve.

And for years as plaster walls cracked
        and steel towers shot up
        as taxis circled the French quarter
        and tankers cut through the industrial canal
        as Uptown accountants raced through red lights
        you lifted eggs from beneath red hens
        entered through the kitchen door.

That morning
> eggshell thoughts stuck to our tongues
> of your escape from rooted pain.
> We swallowed down words of our own.

Still, your keen eyes peer through
> the screen door on Lyons Street
> your silver braid wraps around
> your head as our words drift like down.

Strong stalks crowned in delicate petals
still sing your name.

Creole House

I see a certain grace in the high ceilings and the wide cypress floorboards that run back and forth beneath my feet. Tall windows, flecks and bits in the wavering glass, thick-carved oak mantles, and there, shadows. Seasoned weatherboards overlap, ash-colored shingles shine like tongues, and when I stand in the yard, sink a shovel into the ground to plant a satsuma tree, I dig up a miniature cut glass tea cup, tiny iridescent bottles, shards of china, and green, black, blue chipped marbles that little girls played with beneath the house while their mamma scrubbed and polished the floor with anything she could find, in 1920, and their dad shoved more coal into the fireplace, and the chimney smoked and clouded the sky with faces while a small hand reaches up for the blue marble in my hand.

Trash Day

By the time I got home
my trash can was melted down.
I pulled up in my Toyota truck, sweating
in my dress with the blue and white stripes
I'm told makes me look like a prison mom
and I saw this cruddy green disc by the curb.
I thought someone's car had rolled over it
squashed it flat but when I pulled close
I saw this glob of melted plastic
like an ugly ceramic ashtray
with burnt up black stuff inside
the grass singed brittle, like hair
caught in an oven blaze.
I tried to imagine. Not bums
gathered around burning trash
to keep warm, not in mid-summer
and they would use a metal can.
Maybe the garbage heated up
enough to catch. Or the lid blew off
and a broken beer bottle upside down
with concave bottom caught the sun's light,
an urban magnifying glass like in the cartoons
where, POOF, fire ignites instantly.
What if that white beam caught fire
to a you-may-already-be-a-winner
clearinghouse sweepstake announcement
and this caught another and another and
the whole can blazes
the plastic melts like caramel.
Damn kids, I heard, nothing to do
just wanted to see something burn
but that black smoke swelling upward
must have been extraordinary.

Walking through Palmetto Swamps
    For Olan

Walking through palmetto thick swamps
he whistled loud and shrill.
A feathered soul echoed back
and forth, back and forth they spoke to each other.

I hauled a huge cow skull out
of the vines, lifted it by the eye socket.
He said as a child he collected those
we laughed that one day I might outgrow this.

He offered to carry the skull, but I couldn't bear
for someone else to lug my mud-crusted finds
Later, I wondered why I'm too proud
to share the weight of these bones.

I've never loved like this, he said
never use *love* in a poem, I said
but when he looked away, I cupped my hands around it
afraid the chirping find might fly with the next breeze.

He once tried to bury me with the spiral-fur cat.
Pride flattened in the bottom of my boot
I crawled out of the grave, clawed at his feet
until he let me curl back into his lap.

Will I be in your book? he asked
Never use *book* in a poem, I said
Never use *poem* in a book, he said
I turn the page and he has already
whistled his way in.

Comfort Post-Katrina

It rains hard as I drive
from my new home, Grand Coteau
to the old home, Nouvelle Orleans
past abandoned cities of blue roofs
and the air feels *très triste*.
I stop into *un petite café*
called *Café Tranquille*.
I order, then sit down with
du thé steaming hot and
and I squeeze *du citron* and *du miel*
into my cup. *Doucement*,
I *séparé* the layers
of the *croissent du beurre*
from *la Boulangerie*.
As I swallow, blue roofs disappear,
mud puddles evaporate.
There never was a hurricane,
never was a storm that erased
thousands of neighbors,
no one was
ever named Katrina.
Jamais, jamais.

Dead Woman Winter

Button found a dead body this
morning, a homeless woman. He said he had
met her before, a midget, someone you would
remember. I don't know Button's
real name, like, we haven't worked
together long enough. And he doesn't know
my nick name, like, we haven't known
each other long enough. I can't know what
that feels like, to go from fretting
about small things like hands rough from the dry,
cold air to actually dying outside on the ground
behind the fire station, people in the city passing on foot,
or in cars and they don't know that a shelterless
woman lies dying on the street
with no rescue in sight. All doors stay
locked and electricity flickers off and on.

Today, a child-woman came to
work for us. She said she just got engaged.
At 19 years old, she must complete 43 hours
of public service for her crime. She said
she did something really bad but won't say
what, and I don't ask. She is writing
letters to someone in jail but not the one
she just got engaged to, who she says
her mother hates. Her boyfriend-fiancé,
who she is forbidden to see, will take care
of her, she chirps, though right now
he lives with his parents. We find windows
for her to wash and floors to sweep—we don't
want her to work outside in the killer cold,
this tough and vulnerable girl-woman.

Perched in a chair, she babbles, wants
to show me a picture on her phone of her
boyfriend, but I won't look. I pass to her paper
and clipboard, tell her to list all the things she wanted
to be since a little girl. She litters the paper
with longing: veterinarian, police officer, nurse, baby-
sitter. I wonder how she went from
a baby girl with dreams to a woman who
just wants to be cared for, blankly. I tell her
to pick two careers and write the steps to get
there. To her, I am a torn book, discarded bifocals.
I don't want her to become
the shunned girlfriend, a divorcee,
a lost wife, a roaming woman, wandering
behind a fire station on a bitter night, all doors
shut tight as the unpredictable
winds slip beneath her coat.

Tattoos and Birthmarks

Joe showed me his heart with the dagger, a cross, a swastika, all bleeding like algae on his thick freckled boy arms. *Don't mean nothin'*, he shrugged, bowled the ball down the lane crashing the pins as his pregnant wife drank sprite. *No more pitchers*, she said as she kept score in the little squares. *Take it, Toeper,* Joe handed him the ball.

Toeper held the ball in his right, beer in the left, and an etched eagle drew taut and dark across one shoulder. Toeper launched the ball and sloshed Coors over the lane. *Last pitcher*, the manager scowled as he mopped at the slick.

A scarlet birthmark stained half of Toeper's face. I never heard the name before. Black hair hung straight into his ink eyes, as he told me he swigged his first whiskey at two. His country grandparents laughed, called him *Toeper*, drunk in Choctaw, the only word he still knows, and the grandparents are gone.

At 3:30 a.m. the manager threw us out and Joe's wife cried in the parking lot to keep the keys. I drove Toeper to his house where he pulled his loaded father out of the ditch and stumbled him inside. Toeper led his father to sleep on the kitchen floor, the bed was Toeper's. Driving home, I climbed the bridge, staring into blackness. Coasting down, cars passed me, and I felt like I was in one of those dreams where I can't stop—no brakes, none of us has brakes.

A Reporter who Parties

When you first came home to Louisiana, the country
you never knew, always knew, the land took you in,
lost daughter who can enter the rhythm of any song
a polka, a Texas 2-step—but you really locked into the French Louisiana
waltz, Cajun jitterbug, the zydeco stomp that brings your body to the
new and familiar home.

Curious sister, you sideways watched the cowboys
between songs. Ribbons held your party-time hair, Mardi Gras
hat with bells. But you slowed to investigate the Louisiana
underbelly where Confederate Flags waved on Juneteenth
and you scratched your head and asked and asked again,
trying to write out the truth on your reporter pad.

You travel over ridges of lightness and shadow,
trying to dissect nuanced music that colors this landscape.

Mathew

When the second line funeral parade came pulsing
down St. Ann Street between leaning creole cottages
with the always open shutters and warm stoops
that bordered the steps, when the second line
parade worked its way down the road, umbrellas twirled open
and dancers high-stepped, crossing, uncrossing legs, you
sprung out the door, bottle of whiskey in one hand,
the other hand holding air as you leapt into the middle
of the throbbing cluster of light stepping mourners. Your
white freckled face and orange hair flashed from in the
middle of that pack of black suited dancers, and you
caught the rhythm in your thin body.

Once, after hearing that you had stopped eating,
depressed and drunk in that apartment, I went and
picked you up in my truck, brought you to my house
for spaghetti. For two days we talked and walked
the streets at all hours, and I naively thought I could keep
you from the drinks but you soon broke into the bottles
I didn't remember I even had, liquor that lined
dark cupboards. Finally I agreed to bring you back home.

Years later, you moved to Galveston to be near
ocean, sand, heat. When you called often
to tell me all was well, I knew you were lying,
between jobs, between boyfriends, and
alcohol slurred your words. When you did not call
I believed you were busy, waiting tables,
partying, safe in some man's private home.

When did life become too heavy? Frustration of
never-satisfied body, a heart never whole. You
had to prove what you always believed;
let your unlovable self fall into the forever sleep.

They threw your ashes into the ocean
and dust danced in the rhythms of the winds
in the musical rush of the waves
your spirit still stepping and jazzing
upon the salty breeze.

Lemon Sestina
For Jillian

It's 1:00 a.m, and I am baking a lemon
pound cake, a recipe with too many steps,
the radio plays and, suddenly I hear her voice
the tall woman who once cradled
a ukulele in her strong hands, the year
she collapsed at the movies during Trainwreck.

Sometimes a new recipe makes me a wreck,
squeeze, then zest the lemon
cream the butter and sugar, hands
holding the bowl steady. Each step
calls me closer into a rocking cradle
of music, closer to the low, smoky voice.

Whip the eggs and wonder if he ever voiced
this plan to stalk into the dark auditorium of reckless
laughter, scene of summer ease. Did he cradle
the gun before he aimed at people holding boxes of lemon
drops, junior mints, bags of popcorn, steps
away, just before the blood on his hands.

Who is the heavy-hearted radio host, hand-
somely broadcasting her wavering voice
over the blue city, melancholy tunes steeped
with sweet tea. Is the studio air damp, records
spinning on this summer night, hot lemon breeze?
Does he remember her spirited stride, wooden crates

that held her art books? Timer beeps, take out cake, cradle
onto wire rack, 20 minutes to cool before you handle.
Slice it, taste it. She grew victory gardens, hauled lemons
and satsumas to neighbors, quick chatter of voices.
She played old fashioned songs on the record
player; across pine floors waltzed with long steps.

This cannot last, her muted t-shirt designs, dance steps,
baskets of greens and carrots, vintage dresses. The cradle
wobbles when a lost, dizzy-headed man with a gun wrecks
the summer movie, lets loose on the laughter. Hands
drop popcorn, dark bodies go down, chaotic voices
cry out, ukulele hands grab hold of forever lemons.

The singer two-steps away from the pile of wreckage
montage of last thoughts: lemon grass, padded seats, milk crates
lost recipes, fallen cakes, flickering light, radio static, dark
molasses voices.

Watermelon from the New Orleans Farmers Market

I brought home a watermelon
this morning, laid it on the counter.
As I cut in, it spewed then fell wide
open and I fell back
        to years ago camping in the
        Colorado Rockies where you and Mom
        took us every summer to escape
        the Dallas heat. You wedged a watermelon
        between boulders in a glacial stream,
        light and dark green stripes ran cool
        until you lifted it up
        onto your shoulder, as a father
        carries a small girl through the forest
        our moss-colored eyes keeping careful
        watch for porcupine quills and bobcat paw prints.
        The quick rapping of a red-shafted flicker
        sounded through the pines.

"Pick me a good one," I asked a bronze-skinned
Creole farmer this morning. I did not tap
        but saw tips of your fingers
        thumping green melon backs
        as you listened for the
        watery, ripe music
        in the Dallas Farmers Market.
        Gracias, said a brown-eyed man from The Valley
        you passed him a five and lifted
        the melon to your shoulder
        carried it to the car.

A huge-handed Louisiana man
offered me a moon-round orange meat one,
but I said red, like the Texas melons in my head.
He placed it in my arms, but my shoulders
were too narrow to carry it up high,
my hands still small. I felt the weight
no one here to thump and guide
me through the green sea of water-swollen melons
to nod at the best one.

When I visit your new home
in the Sangre de Cristo mountains
a wedge of watermelon overhangs your plate
at breakfast, and the stereo plays salsa music.
"We'll take our four-mile walk
this afternoon?" you ask.
We lace up our boots then hike up
a high desert trail. Miles later, a counterclockwise
sweep of freetail bats calls in the evening
we answer only with our eyes.

My steps fall just behind yours,
grateful for the comfort of hushed hills.

City of Hey Baby

New Orleans is a city of couch
surfing, slipping in and out
of a friend's house, turning
the key that I have kept in the cup
holder of my car for ten years,
the city where I no longer live
since the storms.

New Orleans is a city of waking
to tense morning traffic over
potholed streets and fragrant corner
coffee shops beckon, please come.

New Orleans is a city of midnight
Port of Call burgers in the joint
where Janis Joplin wails from
the juke box and drooping fishing
nets that never touched seawater
hang from ridged ceilings and
my burger is larger than is good
for me but this hunger calls and calls.

New Orleans is a city of strolling
streets, seeking gifts in cluttered
shops, glancing back and forth
to see who walks behind
or in front of me, watching
for the kind of guy who might
cut my purse strings and run.

New Orleans is a city of flaming
confetti and wide window laughter
that spills onto the sidewalk and years
ago, my dog barked a warning
at 3 a.m., until I awoke, moved

to the living room, found window
pried wide open, a stranger's sneakers
on the couch from feet that
fled low dog bark, feet that
would not fear me.

New Orleans is a City of grease
dripping on the grill at 24-hour
Coops or Clover Grill, city of one
long embrace of a former lover
on a bicycle in the middle of a daiquiri
shop-lined street on an unpredictable day.

New Orleans is the city of "Hey Baby,"
from the coffee shop waitress, the delivery
man, the telephone operator, and "Hey
Baby," from men who follow and men
who don't and "Hey Baby," flies
from balconies and slowing cars because
Hey Baby means nothing and
Hey Baby means too much.

New Orleans is the city where I once
cruised with bicycle boys through
chaotic neighborhoods, over bridges,
narrow sidewalks, cars flying past
and I was the only "girl" in the pack
riding with adult boys who jumped
curbs and made eye contact speaking
to every single person we passed, carefree
as they deterred the hey baby men who
swallowed their words; I rolled forward
in a bubble of maleness that let me cut
through the streets like a shark with no
Hey Babys to be decoded, no need to
consider which is a hey baby push
and which a hey baby kiss.

Patrice Melnick is a writer, arts administrator and community activist.

She is the founder of the Festival of Words, a rural, literary arts organization in Grand Coteau, Louisiana. Melnick taught English and creative writing at Xavier University in New Orleans for thirteen years before moving to Grand Coteau. Patrice Melnick holds a B.A. in English from the University of Texas at Austin, and an M.F.A. in Creative Writing from the University of Alaska, Fairbanks. Her poems and essays have appeared in many literary journals including *Prism International, Red Brick Review* and *Grain*. She has been honored for both her writing and community contributions. Her poem "Tattoos and Birthmarks," was awarded 3rd prize in Federico Garcia Lorca Poetry Prize. She received the Public Humanities Programming award from the Louisiana Endowment for the Humanities and was named one of the Louisianians of 2019 by *Louisiana Life Magazine.*

Patrice Melnick's memoir is entitled *Po-boy Contraband: from Diagnosis Back to Life* (Catalyst Press.) She lives in Grand Coteau with her loving and very patient husband Olan.

www.ingramcontent.com/pod-product-compliance
Lightning Source LLC
LaVergne TN
LVHW040117080426
835507LV00041B/1486